To Step Among Wrack

Hannah and Ian

To Step Among Wrack

Fiona MacInnes

Fiona MacInnes

❖   ❖   ❖

The Orkney Press

The Orkney Press Ltd.,
12 Craigiefield Park,
St Ola, Kirkwall, Orkney

Published 1988
© Fiona MacInnes 1988

Printed in Orkney by
The Kirkwall Press and bound by
Hunter & Foulis Ltd., Edinburgh

The publishers acknowledge subsidy from
The Scottish Arts Council
towards the publication of this volume

ISBN 0 907618 17 0

For Jean and Ian MacInnes

Acknowledgements

Midgarth Road and *Beachcomber* were first published in *The New Shetlander,* Yule 1987.

My sincere thanks to Howie Firth and Archie Bevan.

Contents

Foreword

It is good to see a new talent appearing in Orkney literature. Fiona MacInnes can sketch a landscape with a few vivid words. She sits among the charred heather of the great Hoy hill fire of a few summers ago, and imagines the flame sweeping

> Up the slope to tip the fulmars
> In a hurl from their ledges.

The love of her home islands marks all her poems. Nature's dramas touch her imagination. Some winters ago a wild storm clawed down the shore road that leads to the Stromness kirkyard and Warebeth beach.

> The black furrowed share
> Combing a hill's brow
> Down to the ebb
> Midgarth road
>
> Of the January gales
> Seven years past
> That tore the path into the sea . . .

She can write barbed satirical pieces like *Pretty Poly;* and the times we live in cry out for this kind of writing, too. There is the frenetic taking of snapshots from the train winding slowly through Sutherland.

> As you wangled the waste
> Into right angles
> I'm afraid you forsook
> A rainbow's curve

And lost the day
With the crock of gold
Somewhere stravaiging
The peats of Caithness.

She is against whatever is phoney and show-off and pretentious; thereby, she insists, one misses all that is truly rare and beautiful in life and nature.

One of the loveliest poems in this most promising first collection is *Heather*. To quote from it would be to spoil it. Into one brief simple lyric she packs a great deal of insight into the human heart and its affections and forgettings: a pure act of imagination.

Many new poets imitate and there is nothing wrong in that if, at last, the poet finds his or her own unique voice. Fiona MacInnes imitates nobody. She has brought a wholly fresh original talent to the art of poetry. We may look for even greater treasures to come.

George Mackay Brown

2 May, 1987

To Step Among Wrack

Midgarth Road

I walked this road
At seventeen years
Drystone and ditch
In the shlorich
Wild yellow irises

I came this way
In the springtime of my life
Cheeks red like summer campion
And heart rising with the curlew's cry

I walked the shore road
By saltstone and swell
The black furrowed share
Combing a hill's brow
Down to the ebb

Midgarth Road
Of the January gales
Seven years past
That tore the path into the sea

I remember

And I walk by ochre dykes
In my twenty-fifth year
Weighed by the knowing
That lowers my eyes
To fall by chance on an ancient lichen

Beachcomber

There he goes
That old man
Stretching still to pick up
That one choice piece
Of driftwood for the fire

Turning from the sea
I say 'Lovely night'
'A bit cold now' says he
By the rash and windy blue
Of an early summer eve

There he goes his fat old corgi
Gone from his heels a longtime
Now with stick in hand
More slowly

Treasure

What a droll pun
For the Atlantic to pull
Swirling among the flotsam

All the tales of things that were found
The treasures of the Sou-Westerly
Once it was a ship
With pianos for America

Plinkered among the stones
Spark plugs and pens and a
Cargo of toys . . .
Stories to widen my childish eyes

And now washed up a pallet of biscuits
Snug and sodden
Still in their tins
All over the shore for someone's tea party

Mermaid Butter Cookies

Orkney Winter 82-83

Darkness
The flicker of day
Light and then night
Again. Darkness

Heather

I left the heather behind
Picked on the Rackwick Road
Purple stringy rooty I
Took it back on the boat
To Stromness and
Put it in a jar till
Monday when the *Ola* went
Wanting as many reminders
To make it harder to forget
This summer surging purple
Above the brown rivers in
Spate.
Then
Helmsdale Station
All spruced up
With BR's new look when
I remembered it was sitting
In the kitchen
Left behind
With no thought
The way I always forgot
The island things
About now
As we pass Helmsdale.

Bonfire Night

In wet Edinburgh I caught
The smell of sodden card
And soaking newspaper jam-packed
In the grass topped shelter
At the Attery

The Nessers' stuff was at the Gun. And
We ran over rainy flagstones by
The glinting beacon
Up the Brae
Nearly to Brinkies
We howked our hoard of
Corrugated card.

In the tar black Attery
Were scabby bairns
With gentian violet and
Red armed mothers
Yelling at tea-time from
War time prefabs
No upstairs.

'Hughie Gordon has a gun!'
And we ran past the ratted
Burn that was the boundary
South the Nessers and their
Fisher fathers got the
Fenders for their blaze.

And theirs was always the biggest
On bonfire night.

Debs

I got trapped
Behind a tea-pot in the 'Blue Parrot'
And there was no escaping then

We began to converse
Softly in mumsy tones
To start with

Then it really began to flow
Couched confidently in trivia
Such assurity of class

Chirruping with clipped authority
The cosy references
—'We were only a step from Henley'

The oblivious luxury
Of fine art girls in Edinburgh
Education finishing

Heads turned then
When the laughter clattered
And I caught the mirror

Red faced and 'healthy'
They said, alluding to Peploe
The Glasgow Colourists

What benign amusement when
You said your favourite kitchen tool was
A potato peeler.

We all mocked a little
At eastern humility
The trains to Budapest had lace curtains

Well really?
You had been a trip
With Daddy

And my feet felt muddy
Guilty by association
Trapped there in the window seat

As you took your proper place
Soon everyone knew
And kept their heads down low

The difference resounding
In all the unuttered struggles
The purchases of privilege.

Straight Kate

So that's what becomes
Of people like you
At first, I smiled
At the mould intact
Uncracked

Poor Kate
With her red hair
And her brains
Predestined for clichés
And children's disdain

Hand shooting up
Straight as a rod
Innocent and eager
To be first
To answer

Milk skinned
And glasses
You really had the lot
Porridge and kale
The Protestant kirk

Talking away, it's as if
You were still
Sewing on badges, busy with
Guides, friends with the minister
And his wife.

Such confident surety
And factual security
Make it good to know
There's of course no doubt

That you're off to practise
The Messiah tonight
With your viola
So we're all told.

You coax me into
The girly giggle
Empathising your sexless stoop
And then frankly you begin

To explain the debate
On terrorism;

You dispense the arguments
Weighed and abridged
Consider the exceptions
Evade the controversy

Fuelled by indifference
You continue to assume
My disinterest and ignorance
But never my radicalism

Seeing your chance you
Gently drive home
The inherited morality and
Damning liberalism that comes

So naturally
Without question.

Words

O cruel words
Hurled from my venomous tongue
In a flash
To whip a look
Of such hurt across that loved face
Stunned deeper than all my remorse
O that I could just
Bite my tongue out.

Pretty Poly

Aren't you so O U
Polytechnic lecturer
Channelling forth
A chant of absolutes

Sweet with wide-eyed delight
Flaunting away superfluous skills
Staccato you punctuate OK?
Right! Right then! OK.

Netting the attentive
With flirting smiles
A glance aside
Wearing your casual gear

Like a bearded gnome you
Click with frenetic gestures
Preaching the indubitable benefits
Of speed reading

Memory Improvement
The zealous message
Transferred in coloured felt tip
To fifty flow charts

The Hairdressers

Just like in a palace
The chairs were fiddled into
Fancy swirls white
Metal on the marble floor

As if by sea from a
Spanish terrazza splashed
With red wine and bullfights
A sailor of black and gold

His frilled Contessa
Straight from the Armada
To Stromness in pink velvet
Sunbleached now and in the window

Displaying 'Ellnet'
For professional use only
Among the sweety smell
Of lotions shampoo and conditioner

For the Golf Club dance
Perms and ringlets brushed
And back-combed
Between the driers

All the news and
The goings on
Netted up in a sticky spray
For the Dounby 'Do'

Small girls with hair
Now 'nice and short'
Dangled at regal mirrors
Feeling in fear stubbly necks

And were ushered out
In smarting silence
Of green gaberdine
With collars up

What made it worse
Was everybody else's
Was navy blue handed down
And they got to keep

Their pony tails too
And just to end it all
The marble floor was
Really only lino

The Wind Ensemble

Close clipped beards
On weak chins
Thin nosed
Tight lipped
Lids drooping
And eyebrows arched
To purse a note

From splaykneed
Tight crotched
Black trousered legs
To fingered white
Cravat — Bowed
A peep and a tootle

By plastic bucket chair
To blue rinsed ear
And socked ankled crosslegs
In Glaitness Primary School Gymnasium

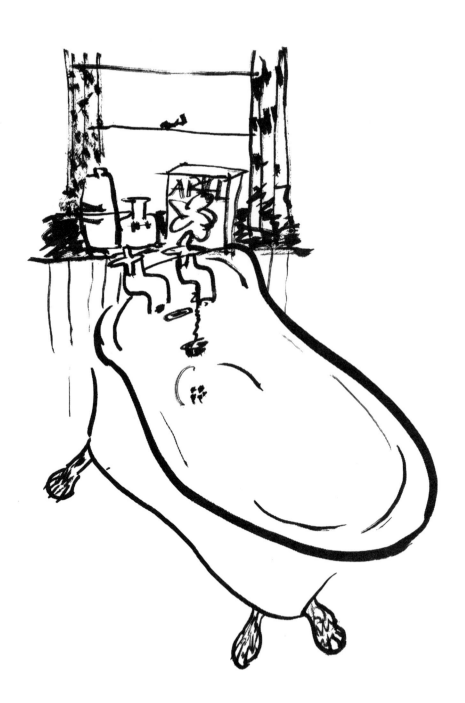

To the Hard Life of Slaters

Twixt Cilla and Charybdis
Suicidal reptile-back
In perilous ascent
From base camp to overflow
Slithers treacherous terrain
Of glacial fibre bath

While predestinator in
The Junta of the Taps
I supervise swilling out
Offending slaters
And send them off
Legging the air
Upside down in
The Great Whirlpool of
The Plughole

Snap Happy

While your camera clicked
Your Praktica missed
The fat morning rabbits
In the sun

As your eyes narrowed
Passing Forsinard
You pared down the deer
Scared through the moss

Squaring off a snap
You backed the stabs
Railing past
Abreast the winter drifts

As you wangled the waste
Into right angles
I'm afraid you forsook
A rainbow's curve

And lost the day
With the crock of gold
Somewhere stravaiging
The peats of Caithness

Hill Fire

Here I sit among the charring
Of last summer's hill fire
The panicked flame that whipped infront
Meek eyed rabbits

Such a burntness the battle field
Of petrified roots stricken
Up the slope to tip the fulmars
In a hurl from their ledges

And now the valley soothing
Scars of grey and barren rock
With gentle salves of green
And soft peat brown water

I wonder today because
The fulmars are back to jostle
A place for their single pointed egg
And I can hear the sea

Pushing a silent cliff. It seems
Far away from the salt sun. This time
The returning green
Among the black

Twilight Zone

It might have been the night
For a song
A slow air
In the time of twilight
And the stooks in rows
Under the bitter moon
Cool below
The sighing pool
Of milk and silver
Where the hills are
Sleeping cold
Carcasses turned
To stone
By welcoming darkness
And like myself
Made immobile
In the spell of twilight.

A fish-box

At the sun set
Where sky and sea
Bled soft in navy

Blue dark the wet
And bruising smear
Of sand made heavy

There the sun
Split in red
Is where I stood

And tides might run
Right over my head
Or tangles flood

At low water
The cutting edge
Of rocks laid bare

Enough to shatter
The looking glass ebb
Gray to shore

To the west
I saw a fish-box
And claimed it mine

Prized the best
Haul the sullen rocks
Would find

I slipped on stone
To reach that place
Where the sun went

And stood alone
Before the race
Here the present

Until light had gone
And the swell insisted
I turned back

For dusk won
Faint resisted
I stepped among wrack
The day done.